Community Helpers

# Helping as a Mentor

by Trudy Becker

FOCUS READERS
PIONEER

www.focusreaders.com



Focus Readers is distributed by North Star Editions:
sales@northstareditions.com | 888-417-0195

Produced for Focus Readers by Red Line Editorial.

Photographs ©: iStockphoto, cover, 1, 8, 11; Shutterstock Images, 4, 7, 12, 15, 17, 18, 21

**Library of Congress Cataloging-in-Publication Data**
Names: Becker, Trudy, author.
Title: Helping as a mentor / Trudy Becker.
Description: Mendota Heights, MN : Focus Readers, [2024] | Series: Community helpers | Includes index. | Audience: Grades 2-3
Identifiers: LCCN 2023026646 (print) | LCCN 2023026647 (ebook) | ISBN 9798889980155 (hardcover) | ISBN 9798889980582 (paperback) | ISBN 9798889981428 (pdf) | ISBN 9798889981015 (ebook)
Subjects: LCSH: Mentoring--Juvenile literature.
Classification: LCC BF637.M45 B43 2024 (print) | LCC BF637.M45 (ebook) | DDC 158.3--dc23/eng/20230721
LC record available at https://lccn.loc.gov/2023026646
LC ebook record available at https://lccn.loc.gov/2023026647

Printed in the United States of America
Mankato, MN
012024

## About the Author

Trudy Becker lives in Minneapolis, Minnesota. She likes exploring new places and loves anything involving books.

# Table of Contents

## Chapter 1

# Spending Time

A woman and a girl get ice cream. They take their ice cream to a park. Then they sit on a bench together. They talk about the girl's life.

These people are not family. The woman is a **mentor**. She spends time with the younger girl. She helps the girl have **experiences**. She also talks to the girl about life and feelings.

**Did You Know?**

Mentors help connect people in a **community**.

## Chapter 2

# What Are Mentors?

Mentors play a big role in a community. Mentors help **guide** other people. Usually, mentors are older. They help younger people.

Younger people may not have much money. They might have fewer chances to do things. With mentors, they can learn new things. They can gain **confidence**, too.

**Did You Know?**

Mentors can be **role models**. They show younger people how to act.

Chapter 3

# What Mentors Do

Mentor pairs can do many things together. They might visit museums. They might go to libraries. Some pairs might play games together.

Mentors can help with schoolwork, too. They might teach reading skills. They might help with writing or speaking. Sometimes mentors also help with computer skills.

**Did You Know?**

Some pairs meet very often. Some meet once in a while.

# Finding Matches

Sometimes groups set up mentor pairs. They find good matches. Then the pairs can start to meet. The groups can also suggest **activities**. Sometimes pairs are not a good match. So, the groups can help. They can find new partners.

Chapter 4

# Giving Advice

Mentors often help by talking. They give **advice**. They might have ideas for their partners. But mentors must also listen carefully. That way, they can offer useful help.

Younger partners feel support from their mentors. They might have fewer worries. They can learn, too. Then the whole community gets better.

**Did You Know?**

Some people have mentors when they are young. Later, they become mentors.

FOCUS ON

# Helping as a Mentor

*Write your answers on a separate piece of paper.*

1. Write a sentence that explains the main idea of Chapter 4.
2. If you had a mentor, what would you want to do with them? Why?
3. What do mentor groups help with?
   A. deciding everything partners do
   B. matching mentors with partners
   C. telling mentors not to talk
4. Why might a mentor's advice be useful?
   A. The mentor has had more experiences.
   B. The mentor doesn't know the partner's life.
   C. The mentor is good at making things up.

*Answer key on page 24.*

# Glossary

**activities**
Things that people can do.

**advice**
Ideas about what someone should do.

**community**
A group of people and the places where they spend time.

**confidence**
The feeling that you can do something well.

**experiences**
New things that people get to do.

**guide**
To help lead someone to do something.

**mentor**
A person who spends time with a younger person and helps them learn.

**role models**
People who others look up to as examples.

# To Learn More

## BOOKS

Leaf, Christina. *Museum*. Minneapolis: Bellwether Media, 2023.

Ventura, Marne. *Government and Community*. Minneapolis: Abdo Publishing, 2019.

## NOTE TO EDUCATORS

Visit **www.focusreaders.com** to find lesson plans, activities, links, and other resources related to this title.

# Index



**Answer Key: 1.** Answers will vary; **2.** Answers will vary; **3.** B; **4.** A